D0975907

Smithsonian

LITTLE EXPLORER

# TRICERATOPS

by Janet Riehecky

CAPSTONE PRESS
a capstone imprint

Little Explorer is published by Capstone Press,
1710 Roe Crest Drive, North Mankato, Minnesota 56003
www.capstoneyoungreaders.com

**Library of Congress
Cataloging-in-Publication Data**
Riehecky, Janet, 1953– author.
Triceratops / by Janet Riehecky.
pages cm. — (Smithsonian little explorer.
Little paleontologist)
Summary: "Introduces young readers to Triceratops,
including physical characteristics, diet, habitat, and life
cycle"— Provided by publisher.
Audience: Ages 4–7.
Audience: K to grade 3.
Includes index.
ISBN 978-1-4914-0811-7 (library binding)
ISBN 978-1-4914-0823-0 (paperback)
ISBN 978-1-4914-0817-9 (paper over board)
ISBN 978-1-4914-0829-2 (eBook PDF)
1. Triceratops—Juvenile literature. 2. Dinosaurs—Juvenile
literature. I. Title.
QE862.O65R5565 2015
567.915'8—dc23

2014001860

**Editorial Credits**
Michelle Hasselius, editor; Heidi Thompson and
Kazuko Collins, designers; Wanda Winch, media
researcher; Kathy McColley, production specialist

Our very special thanks to Mike Brett-Surman, PhD,
Museum Specialist for Fossil Dinosaurs, Reptiles,
Amphibians, and Fish at the National Museum of
Natural History, Smithsonian Institution, for his
curatorial review. Capstone would also like to thank
Kealy Wilson, Product Development Manager, and the
following at Smithsonian Enterprises: Ellen Nanney,
Licensing Manager; Brigid Ferraro, Vice President,
Education and Consumer Products; Carol LeBlanc,
Senior Vice President, Education and Consumer Products.

**Image Credits**
Capstone: James Field, 25 (bottom), Steve Weston, 13;
Corbis: Jonathan Blair, 8, Paul A. Souders, 23 (b); Creatas,
6; Dreamstime: Peterpolak, 12; Jon Hughes, cover, 1,
4–7, 9, 11, 14, 15, 16–17, 19, 28–29; Library of Congress:
Prints and Photographs Division, 22 (top); Shutterstock:
BACO, 4 (bus), Chris Fourie, 10, Computer Earth, 20–21,
30–31, Horse Crazy, 17 (top right), leonello calvetti, 2–3,
4 (bottom left), Linda Bucklin, 24 (top), Mahathir Mohd
Yasin, 26–27, Michael Rosskothen, 24 (b), 25 (t), Ozja, 27
(b), reallyround, 5 (tr), SebastialKaul, 28 (b), Simon_g, 18,
Steffen Foerster, 5 (tl), T4W4, 4 (folder), The_Pixel, 22–23

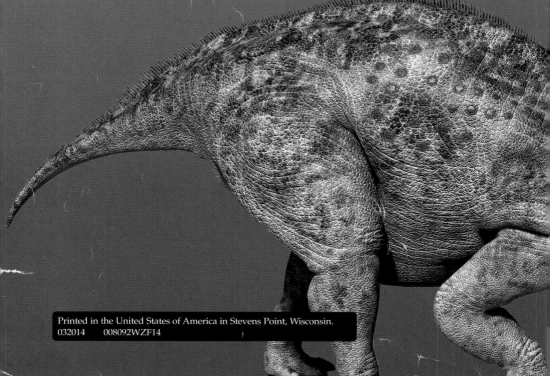

Printed in the United States of America in Stevens Point, Wisconsin.
032014    008092WZF14

# TABLE OF CONTENTS

name: Triceratops

how to say it: try-SAIR-uh-tops

when it lived: Cretaceous Period, Mesozoic Era

what it ate: plants

size: 25 to 30 feet (7.6 to 9.1 meters) long
9 to 10 feet (2.7 to 3 m) tall
weighed 6 to 12 tons
(5.4 to 11 metric tons)

# Thanks to FOSSILS

A fossil is evidence of life from the past. Fossils of things like bones, teeth, and tracks found in the earth have taught us everything we know about dinosaurs.

Triceratops roamed North America 68–66 million years ago. Most people know what Triceratops looked like. Its huge head and bony frill make it hard to miss!

# A STRANGE-LOOKING DINOSAUR

Triceratops means "three-horned face." The dinosaur looked a little like a rhinoceros. Some people even call Triceratops a prehistoric rhinoceros. But the two animals are not related.

short tail

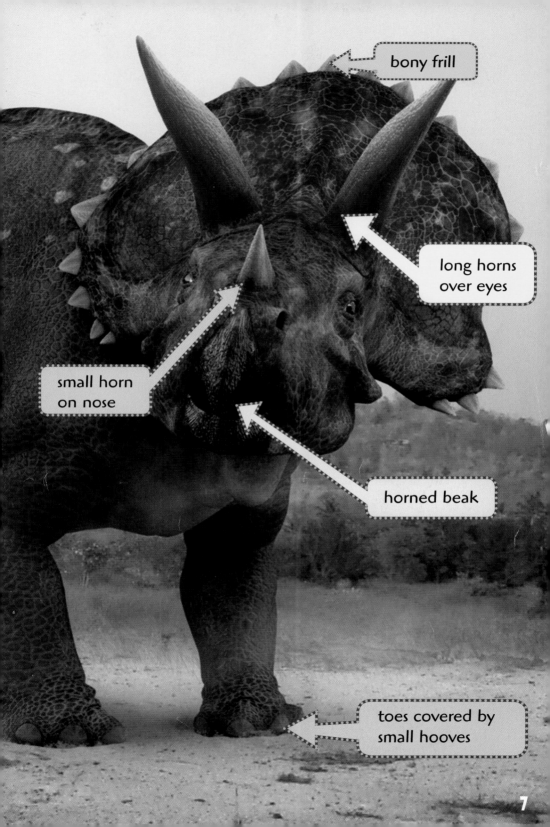

bony frill

long horns
over eyes

small horn
on nose

horned beak

toes covered by
small hooves

# GROWING UP

Triceratops hatched from an egg. The baby had large eyes and a short frill.

A young Triceratops' horns curved back. Triangle-shaped spikes grew on the edge of its frill.

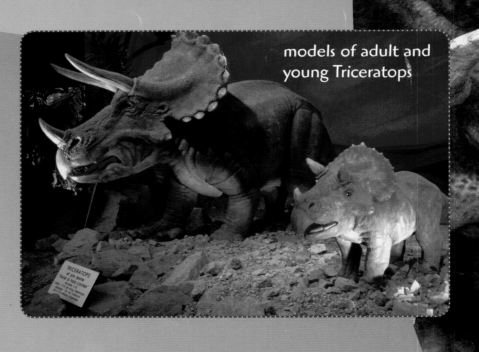

models of adult and young Triceratops

When Triceratops became an adult, its horns changed direction. They curved forward. The spikes on its frill smoothed together.

Triceratops' skull was up to 8 feet (2.4 m) long.

# A THRILLING FRILL

Triceratops' frill was used for different things:

✔ The frill likely protected Triceratops during an attack.

✔ A male may have used his big frill to attract a female Triceratops.

✔ The frill also may have kept Triceratops cool. Heat from the dinosaur's body could escape off the wide frill.

Elephants use their ears to cool off in the same way.

# MIGHTY HORNS

Below its two long horns, Triceratops had a shorter horn on its nose.

A male Triceratops probably locked horns with other males during battles over a mate.

A female Triceratops likely wanted a mate with long horns. Long horns showed strength and power.

Horns helped Triceratops fight
if it was attacked. They were
sharp enough to stab a predator.

# DEFENDING ITSELF

Triceratops was good at protecting itself and its young. A group of Triceratops could have stood shoulder to shoulder. The young were protected behind the wall. No predator could get through the strong wall they made.

If Triceratops charged, even a Tyrannosaurus rex would have been in trouble.

*"No species that has ever evolved on land could withstand the full charge of such an animal."*
—paleontologist Robert Bakker

# STANDING TALL

Scientists used to think Triceratops'
legs stuck out on both sides, like
a crocodile's. Now they think
the dinosaur's legs were almost
upright. Its legs moved forward and
backward in nearly a straight line.

Triceratops could also
lock its knees. Its legs
wouldn't bend at all.

Many scientists think
Triceratops could run
10 to 15 miles per hour
(16 to 24 kilometers per hour).

Horses and cows lock their knees to sleep standing up. Triceratops might have done this too.

# WHAT'S FOR DINNER?

Triceratops was an herbivore. That means it ate plants. With its short neck, Triceratops had to eat plants that grew close to the ground.

parrot

The dinosaur had a parrotlike beak for a mouth. It could chomp through hard foods, like conifer needles and branches. Triceratops also grazed on ferns, cycads, and flowering plants.

Triceratops had up to 800 teeth in its mouth. If Triceratops lost a tooth, a new one grew in. It had three to five replacement teeth underneath each tooth.

# TRICERATOPS' WORLD

Triceratops lived during the end of the Cretaceous
Period. The world was warmer during this time.
Evergreen conifers, ferns, and cycads covered
the land. Flowering plants grew for the first time.

Many scientists think Triceratops lived on wide,
flat plains. It also looked for food in the forests.

The Cretaceous Period lasted from 145 million to 66 million years ago.

# DINOSAUR ERA

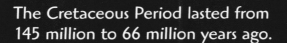

| TRIASSIC | JURASSIC | CRETACEOUS | |
|---|---|---|---|

250        200        145        66        present

millions of
years ago

The average temperature was a few degrees warmer than today.

A shallow sea covered the middle of North America.

# DISCOVERY

The first Triceratops fossil was a pair of horns. They were found outside Denver, Colorado, in 1887.

Othniel Marsh

Canada
Montana
Wyoming
South Dakota
Utah
Colorado

Triceratops fossils have been discovered in Alberta and Saskatchewan, Canada. Colorado, Montana, South Dakota, Wyoming, and Utah also have Triceratops fossils.

The horns were sent to paleontologist Othniel Marsh. He thought they were from a bison. Later more fossils were found. Marsh knew they were from a dinosaur. He named it Triceratops.

More than 100 Triceratops skulls have been found.

# TRICERATOPS RELATIVES

Triceratops was part of a group of dinosaurs called the ceratopsians. These dinosaurs all had horns and frills.

### Pentaceratops

(pen-tuh-SAIR-uh-tops)
had a short horn on its
nose. The horns over
its eyes were long. Its
frill had many short spikes.

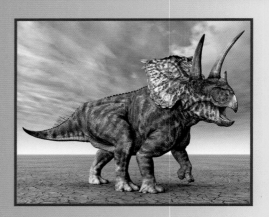

### Diabloceratops

(dee-ah-bloh-SAIR-uh-tops)
was discovered recently.
It had short horns over its
eyes and on its nose. Two
long spikes grew out of the
top of its frill.

**Centrosaurus**
(sen-tro-SOR-us)
had a long horn on
its nose. It had very
short horns over its
eyes. Its frill had small
spikes. Two of these
spikes curled forward.

**Styracosaurus**
(sty-rak-oh-SAWR-us)
had a long horn on
its nose, but no horns
above the eyes. The
frill had at least four
long spikes.

# DID YOU KNOW?

Triceratops is the official state dinosaur of Wyoming. It is also the official fossil of South Dakota.

Triceratops had one of the largest skulls ever. It was almost one-third of its body.

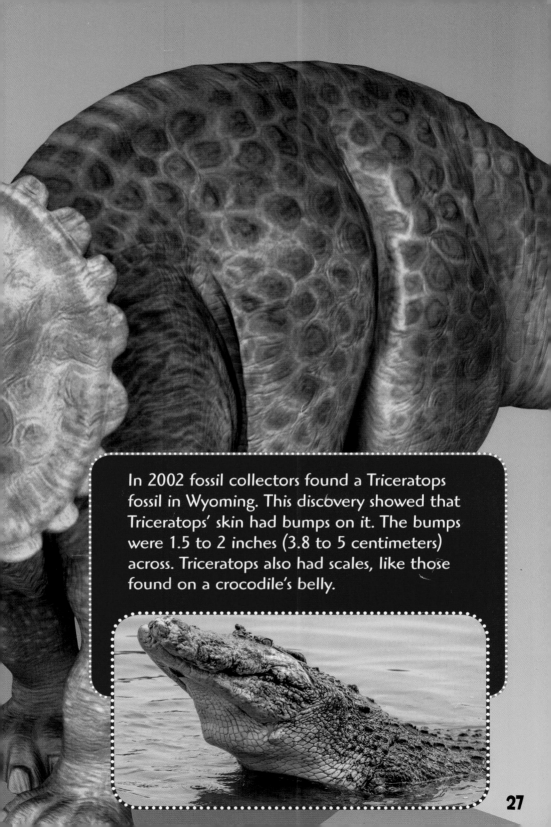

In 2002 fossil collectors found a Triceratops fossil in Wyoming. This discovery showed that Triceratops' skin had bumps on it. The bumps were 1.5 to 2 inches (3.8 to 5 centimeters) across. Triceratops also had scales, like those found on a crocodile's belly.

# EXTINCTION

Many scientists think an asteroid hit Earth 66 million years ago. The asteroid probably caused the dinosaurs to become extinct.

The asteroid would have thrown enough dirt into the air to block the sunlight. Plants and animals can't live without sunlight.

Scientists think the asteroid that hit Earth was 6 miles (9.7 km) wide!

The crash could also have started
deadly earthquakes and tsunamis.

Triceratops was one of the
last Mesozoic dinosaurs to
become extinct.

# GLOSSARY

**asteroid**—a large rock that travels through space

**attract**—to get the attention of something or someone

**conifer**—a tree with cones and narrow leaves called needles

**cycad**—a plant shaped like a tall pineapple, with a feathery crown of palmlike leaves

**earthquake**—a very strong shaking or trembling of the ground

**extinct**—no longer living or existing

**fern**—a plant with long, thin leaves known as fronds

**fossil**—evidence of life from the geologic past

**frill**—a large, bony plate that grows from the back of the skull

**mate**—the male or female partner of a pair animals

**Mesozoic Era**—the age of dinosaurs, which includes the Triassic, Jurassic, and Cretaceous periods; when the first birds, mammals, and flowers appeared

**paleontologist**—a scientist who studies fossils

**predator**—an animal that hunts other animals for food

**tsunami**—a very large wave

# CRITICAL THINKING USING THE COMMON CORE

Triceratops had a large frill on his head. Describe three ways the dinosaur used its frill. (Key Ideas and Details)

Turn to page 13. What is happening in this picture? Use the text to help you with your answer. (Integration of Knowledge and Ideas)

Paleontologist Othniel Marsh discovered the first Triceratops fossil in 1887. What is a fossil? (Craft and Structure)

# READ MORE

**Bailey, Gerry.** *Triceratops*. Smithsonian Prehistoric Zone. New York: Crabtree Pub., 2011.

**Bolte, Mari.** *Triceratops: Three-Horned Giant.* First Graphics. North Mankato, Minn.: Capstone Press, 2012.

**Mara, Wil.** *Triceratops*. New York: Children's Press, 2012.

# INTERNET SITES

FactHound offers a safe, fun way to find Internet sites related to this book. All of the sites on FactHound have been researched by our staff.

Here's all you do:

Visit *www.facthound.com*

Type in this code: 9781491408117

Check out projects, games and lots more at
**www.capstonekids.com**

# INDEX